THE HOW AND WHY WONDER BOOK OF
STARS

By Norman Hoss

Illustrated by James Ponter

Edited under the supervision of

Dr. Paul E. Blackwood
Specialist for Elementary Science
U. S. Department of Health, Education and Welfare
Washington, D. C.

Text and illustrations approved by

Oakes A. White
Brooklyn Children's Museum
Brooklyn, New York

SCHOOL EDITION

Charles E. Merrill Books, Inc.

By special arrangement with Wonder Books, Inc.

INTRODUCTION

This book about stars is one in a series of *How and Why* books planned to open doors of scientific knowledge to young readers. It has been prepared to help young people explore, in a systematic way, the wonders of the universe. It will help them discover what astronomers — both ancient and modern — have learned and stimulate children to raise new and unanswered questions. This is in the true spirit of science.

Exploring the stars has always been fascinating to people everywhere. Perhaps this is because our neighbors in the sky are so much a part of everyone's experience. Everyone can look up and behold the heavens. Yet "just looking" does not tell us all we want to know about the untold thousands of galaxies and the unimaginable vastness of space. Thus we are left with a sense of wonder and awe. It has always been so.

But if "just looking" at the stars does not give us all the answers to our questions, then we must turn to the vast store of knowledge gathered by the astronomers. They have used special instruments and mathematics as well as their experienced eyes to get answers, and much of what they have learned is contained in the following pages.

This book will enable young people to observe the heavens with increased respect for what is known, and greater appreciation for what is yet unknown.

Paul E. Blackwood
Specialist for Elementary Science
U. S. Department of Health, Education and Welfare
Washington, D. C.

Contents

LIGHTS IN THE SKY

If you look up at the sky on a clear night, what do you see? There are thousands of lights against a dark background. Let's pretend at first that we know nothing but what we can see. Then it will be easy to understand what people first thought about these lights in the sky and how they slowly pieced together the wonderful facts and ideas that make up the science of astronomy.

What can we see in the sky?

Let's say that we are standing in a place where there are no buildings or trees or mountains to block our view of the sky, for instance on the deck of a ship in the ocean. The sky will look to us the same as it looked to the earliest man on earth. In thousands of years there have been no changes that you could tell by just looking.

Beyond our ship all we can see is water and sky. It is as if we were alone in an empty house. The shape of the house looks very simple. The surface of the ocean makes the floor. It appears to be flat and perfectly round. We seem to be exactly in the center of it. The house appears to be covered by a dome. It is as if the sky were a half of a hollow

ball, a great bowl turned upside down on a flat disk which is the earth. Looking all around us we can see where the sky and earth seem to meet in a circle. We name this circle the horizon.

As we look up from the horizon in any direction, there are the lights of the stars in the dome of the sky. On some nights the moon appears and the fainter stars.fade from view. On dark nights a band of milky light extends across part of the sky. By day the blinding light of the sun is all we can see in the sky.

This is the way the universe looked to primitive people, and so it is the way they believed it to be. They believed the earth was flat, because it looks flat. They believed the horizon was the edge of the earth, because you can't see anything beyond it. And they believed that the sky was the dome-shaped roof of the world.

What did primitive people believe about the sky?

Some thought that the stars were lights attached to the sky, just as we have electric lights in the ceiling of a room. Others believed there was a bright heaven beyond the sky and that the stars were holes in the dome letting in light from heaven.

This was man's first idea of the universe (a word that includes everything that exists). We now know these early beliefs are not true, but they were based on what could be seen. If there were no one to tell us what men have learned, we would start with this same view of the universe.

Ancient people were not satisfied with this description of the "how" of the stars. They wanted to explain the "why." In trying to do this they made up stories called myths about gods and heroes. There were many myths about the sky among people in different places at different times. Myths tried to explain such things as why the sun rises and sets and why the moon appears to change shape from night to night.

What do myths tell of the sky?

5

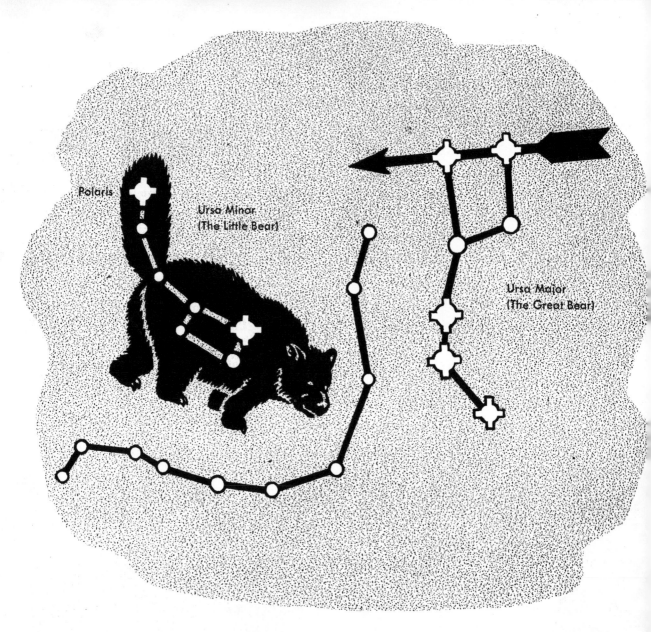

Naming the patterns of stars helped people remember them and use them to find their way at night. Notice how the "pointer stars" in Ursa Major help you find the North Star, Polaris.

We are not interested in the explanations that myths give for what happens in the sky. We read myths nowadays because some of them are beautiful stories that tell deep truths about human nature. In this book we are interested in myths for only one reason. They provided a map of the sky, which, with some changes, astronomers still use today.

When you look at the stars the first thing you notice is that some are brighter than others. Then you notice that some of the bright ones make patterns that are easy to remember. These patterns of stars are called constellations. The ancient Greeks gave them names and made up myths about them. By naming the con-

What are constellations?

stellations, they created a map of the sky. Just as a map of the United States shows that Chicago is in Illinois, the map of the constellations shows that Polaris, the North Star, is in the constellation Ursa Minor, the Little Bear. Don't expect to recognize the constellations from the creatures they are named for. The star maps in the back of the book show the constellations.

As soon as men recognized a pattern of stars as a constellation, they were able to make a great discovery. The stars move. A single constellation can be found in different parts of the sky at different times. But the patterns themselves never change; all the stars seem to move together. It seemed obvious to ancient men that the sky itself moved and all the stars were attached to it. But were they all? As men watched the sky they discovered that a few of the brightest stars did not stay in a particular constellation. At different times of the year they could be seen in different constellations. These lights were called wanderers. From the Greek word for "wanderer" we get our word *planet*.

There were five planets that the Greeks

How were the planets named? could see, and they named them after gods (we now use their Roman names): Jupiter, the ruler of the gods; Venus, the goddess of love; Mars, the god of war; Mercury, the messenger of the gods; and Saturn, Father Time.

The ancient watchers of the sky also saw that sometimes there were lights that blazed across the sky and disappeared. These were thought to be stars that had fallen from the sky.

There was one other thing that ancient people sometimes saw in the sky, a bright light with a long shining tail. These comets, as they are called, appeared many years apart. Ordinarily no one sees more than one in his lifetime. Up until recent times many people were terrified when a comet appeared. Sometimes they thought the end of the world had come.

Everything, then—except man-made satellites—that we can see in the sky today with our eyes alone was known to ancient men: sun, moon, stars, the Milky Way, planets, meteors (which is the name we now give to the "falling stars"), and comets.

When comets such as this appeared in the sky, ancient people were frightened.

EARTH AND SKY

By the sixth century B.C., in Greece,

When did men first guess the earth was round? there were men calling themselves philosophers who tried to explain the facts of nature without using the stories of mythology.

From the fact that sun, moon and stars set in the west and then rise in the east the next day, these men reasoned that everything in the sky must go around the earth every day. They also noted that some stars to the north never set, but move in circles around

As a boat moves away, its sail seems to "sink" below the horizon. This shows that the earth is curved.

the North Star, Polaris. It seemed clear to them that the sky was not a bowl, a half of a ball, as it appeared to primitive men. They pictured it as a whole ball, a hollow sphere.

In science, one idea leads to another, and the idea of the celestial sphere, as the ball of the sky was called, led to a more important discovery. If the sky is a sphere, philosophers reasoned, it would seem proper that the earth is also shaped like a ball. This idea was taught by a few philosophers as early as the fifth century B.C. This was two thousand years before Ferdinand Magellan's

ships proved the earth was round by sailing around it.

Learned men called attention to familiar facts that showed the earth was curved. When a ship disappears over the horizon, they pointed out, its mast remains visible for a time after the hull has gone out of sight, just as if the ship were going over a hill.

More than two centuries before Christ, a Greek named Eratosthenes, librarian of the great museum in Alexandria, Egypt, actually figured the distance around the earth with near-perfect accuracy.

With the work of the great astronomer

How did ancient astronomers picture the universe?

Ptolemy, who lived in Alexandria in the second century A.D., the ancient view of the universe was completed. It is shown in the model. At the center is the globe of the earth. Around it is the bigger globe of the celestial sphere. Its axis (the line on which it turns) runs through the center of the earth. The stars are fixed to the sphere, so that as it rotates from east to west, the stars turn with it, going once around the earth every twenty-four hours.

This view of the universe explained the motions of the stars satisfactorily, even though it was not correct. This often happens in science. But one thing Ptolemy was unable to explain was the motions of the planets. He made up a remarkably clever — and complicated — picture of how the planets move, but it did not quite fit the facts. Ptolemy was wrong on two vital counts. He thought the earth was the center of the universe

Although we can't feel it, the earth is hurtling through space.

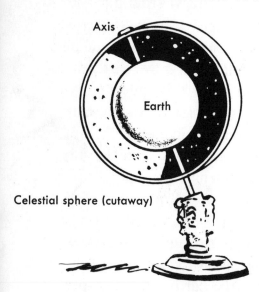

Celestial sphere (cutaway)

Axis

Earth

A model of the ancient idea of the universe

and he thought that the earth stood still while everything else moved around it.

Curiously enough one man had the right answers on these two points some 500 years before Ptolemy. A philosopher named Aristarchus suggested that the apparent movement of the stars is caused by the earth turning on its axis. And he even suggested that the earth moves around the sun. It is not surprising that his ideas were ignored. It is hard to believe that we are riding on a spinning space ship zipping around the sun.

ASTRONOMY AND ASTROLOGY

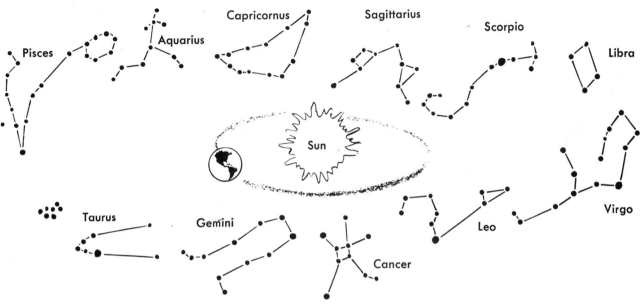

Twelve constellations form a circle in the sky known as the Zodiac. As the earth moves around the sun, the sun appears to rise and set in a part of the sky marked by one after another of these constellations.

SO THE ancient view of the universe remained unchanged and unquestioned for some 1,500 years. You might think that people simply lost interest in the stars, but this was not true. Some men throughout the Middle Ages watched the sky with deep interest. They did not make discoveries as the Greeks had, because they were not interested in astronomy. They were interested in astrology.

What is astrology? Astrology was an ancient system of magic. Astrologers thought they could tell what was going to happen by studying the positions of the sun, moon, and planets. Astrology was based on the fact that the courses of these bodies are confined to a narrow band of the sky. This band was named the Zodiac and was divided into twelve parts called signs. The signs were named for the constellations in those twelve regions of the sky. Because of a "wobble" in the earth's motion the constellations are no longer seen in the signs bearing their names. But there are still people who believe in astrology.

Unless you carefully study the sky and apply mathematics to what you see, it is just as easy to believe the ideas of astrology as the facts of astronomy. Before people came to trust the methods of science, they saw no reason to accept what astronomers told them. Astronomy deals with facts that are not apparent in everyday life. You can't bring a star into a laboratory — you can only study its light.

THE SOLAR SYSTEM

Nicolaus Copernicus

WE SHOULD NOT be surprised that the first attempt to change the ancient view of the universe met with strong opposition. Nicolaus Copernicus, a Polish monk, was the first to disagree publicly with the accepted scheme. His book was not published until a few days before his death in 1543, so the task of defending his ideas fell to others.

How did Copernicus change men's view of the universe?

After studying the planets for years, Copernicus concluded that their motions could be explained only one way. He decided that the earth itself is one of the planets and that they all move around the sun. He was unable to prove his plan, because observations of the sky were so inaccurate at the time. But he did work out the correct order of the planets in distance from the sun.

It was the great Italian scientist Galileo who bore the brunt of defending the Copernican system. With the aid of the newly invented telescope, he was able to add additional evidence for the new system and he wrote eloquently in defense of it. He was finally imprisoned for teaching it. Old and ill, he was forced to deny that the earth moved around the sun. But his work had already been done. Copernicus' view of the universe had been taken up by more and more of the growing number of scientists.

It was the patient observations of the Danish astronomer Tycho Brahe that made it possible finally to work out an accurate picture of the solar system, as the sun and its planets are called. From Brahe's long series of precise observations, Johann Kepler in 1609 figured out that the paths of the planets around the sun were not circles, as Copernicus had assumed. Kepler found the orbits are slightly flattened circles — a figure that is known as an ellipse. The illustration and caption show a simple way to draw an ellipse. The sun is located in this figure at one of the two points known as focuses which are indicated in the illustration by the tacks.

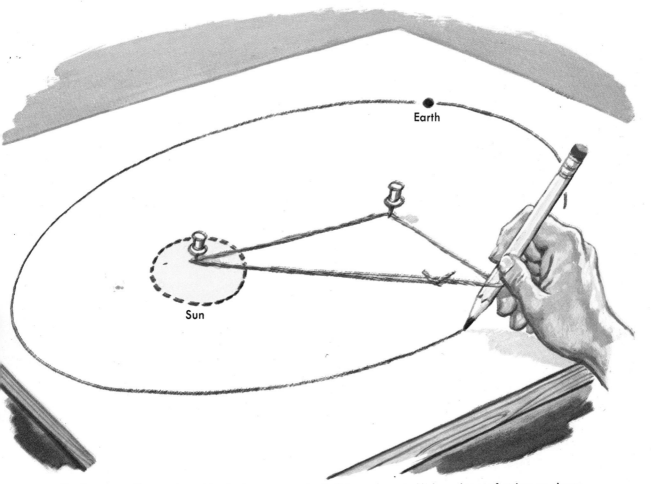

Earth

Sun

To draw an ellipse, place two tacks a convenient distance apart. Make a loop of string as shown. The larger the loop is, the bigger the ellipse. Put a pencil through the loop and draw the string snug. If you keep the loop tight, the pencil can move in only one path. This path is an ellipse. The closer the tacks are together, the more like a circle the ellipse will look.

It then remained for Isaac Newton to explain why the planets move in this pattern and what keeps the whole solar system in its pattern. He stated that every piece of matter attracts every other piece. This force he called gravity. He did not try to say what gravity is, but he showed by mathematics exactly how it works. The pull of gravity between two objects is greater the "heavier" they are — that is, the more "mass" they have. The attraction increases the closer together objects are.

What holds the solar system together?

It would be interesting to continue to follow the story, step by step, of how men have pieced together their knowledge of the skies, but this would require a huge book. Since the time of Newton, more and more scientists have made more and more discoveries. The rest of this book tells about the universe as scientists now know it. Once we have seen that the earth is not the center of the universe, we no longer have to study the heavenly bodies only as they appear from the earth. We can imagine that we are looking at them from any spot in space that gives us the best view.

Sir Isaac Newton

THE SUN

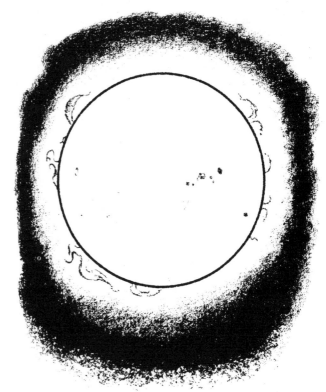

The sunspots shown are huge storms covering areas larger than the earth's diameter. The flares around the edge are great eruptions of fiery gases thousands of miles long.

W E SHALL naturally look first at the sun, then at the sun's family of planets, of which our earth is a member. The family is called the solar system, from the Latin word *solus,* for sun.

Throughout all the centuries, up until man first released atomic energy in the 1940's, the sun has been earth's only power plant. All the usable energy on earth has come from the sun. When primitive man burned a log of wood, he was releasing energy from the sun's rays stored in the wood by the processes of life in the tree. The energy from the food we eat can be traced to the sun in the same way. Electricity produced by water falling over a dam is energy from the sun because the sun's heat had to raise up the water by evaporation before it could fall back to the earth as rain and run down the rivers.

For centuries men wondered how the sun could continue to put out so much heat energy

Why doesn't the sun burn up?

without burning up. The answer we now know is that the sun does not burn. It is an atomic-energy furnace that produces its energy by the same process as the hydrogen bomb. The immediate question that arises is: "Why doesn't the sun blow up like a hydrogen bomb?" And the answer is: because it is so big. Remember, Newton discovered that every particle of matter attracts every other particle. In the sun there are so many atoms that their attraction for each other is strong enough to resist the fantastic forces — greater than those in the hydrogen bomb—that are thrusting atoms apart.

15

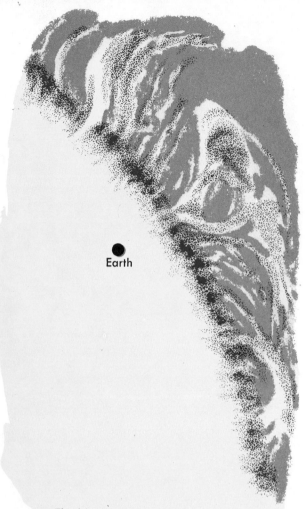

The black spot represents the size of the earth against the surface of the sun.

The sun must be made of lighter stuff than the earth. If the earth were as big as the sun, it would weigh four times as much.

The reason is that the sun is all gas. It **What is the sun made of?** may be hard to imagine a ball of gas in space. We think of gas as a substance that escapes unless we keep it closed in, like the gas in a toy balloon. But again, it is gravity that holds the gas together in the sun, just as the gravity of the earth holds its layer of air around it. The gravity of the sun is vastly greater than that of the earth. The attraction of the sun's atoms toward its center compresses them so much that a piece from the middle of the sun would be heavier than a block of iron the same size. Yet the center of the sun has not been squeezed into a solid core or even into liquid. It is so hot in the sun that nothing can exist as a solid or liquid.

If the sun, a super hydrogen bomb, is **How big is the sun?** so big that it cannot blow itself up, then obviously its size is hard to imagine in terms of earthly measurements. The sun is more than a million times bigger than the earth. Its diameter is 864,000 miles as compared with the earth's 7,927 miles. But the sun is not nearly a million times heavier than the earth. Its mass is only about 332,000 times as great as the earth's. (The word "only" sounds funny with a figure that, in terms of weight on the surface of the earth, would mean 4,380,000,000,000,-000,000,000,000,000 pounds.)

The heat at the center of the sun is estimated at about 35,000,**How hot is the sun?** 000 degrees on the same kind of Fahrenheit scale that the weatherman uses. Outward from the center the temperature grows gradually lower. At the "surface," the face of the sun from which we get our heat, it is only 11,000 degrees. (There's that word "only" again. About the hottest thing we can think of on earth is the inside of a steel-making furnace. The sun's face is many times hotter.)

THE PLANETS

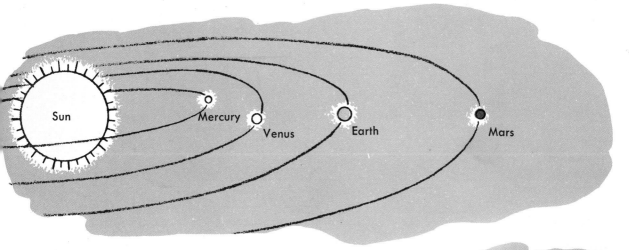

If we could stand in outer space we

How do the planets shine?

could see tiny specks of light around the great blazing ball of the sun. These are the planets. They do not give off light of their own. We can see them only by sunlight reflected from them.

We now know of nine planets; one of these is our earth. Of the other eight, four are very like the earth — globes of rock of comparable size. The other four are giants compared with the earth and they are made of much lighter stuff. Mercury, Venus, Mars and Pluto are called terrestrial planets (from the Latin word for earth), because they are like the earth. The giant planets are Jupiter, Saturn, Uranus and Neptune.

The Greeks called the planets wanderers because they didn't understand the way they move. Actually the sun's family is very well behaved. All the planets move in a regular pattern.

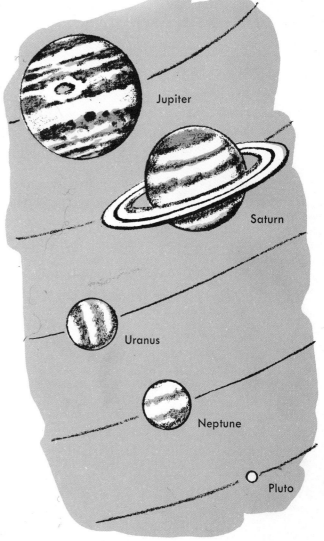

The comparative sizes of the sun and planets and their distances apart cannot be shown in one picture. This is because the sun is so tremendously bigger than the planets, and the distances between the planets are so vast compared with their sizes. The relative sizes and distances are shown in separate pictures on page 19.

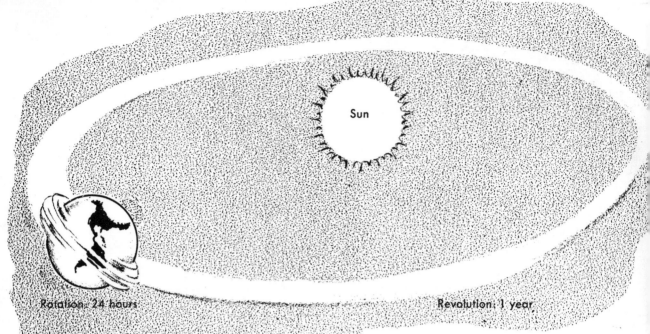

Sun

Rotation: 24 hours

Revolution: 1 year

The earth rotates on its axis once a day.
It revolves around the sun once a year.

The planets all move around the sun in
the same direction.
This motion is called
revolution, and we
say a planet *revolves* in its orbit — its
path around the sun. In addition, the
planets spin like tops. This motion is
called rotation, and we say a planet
rotates on its axis — an imaginary line
through its center. Although we cannot actually see some of the planets rotate, there are convincing reasons to believe that they all rotate in the same direction as the earth does. (The planet
Uranus is a special case, because it is
"tipped over" so that its north pole
points almost at the center of the sun.)
The sun also rotates, but more slowly
than most of the planets. It takes twenty-
five days to turn once around.

Astronomers tell us that the orbits
of all the planets lie almost in the same
plane. To picture what this means, imagine that you are making a model of

**How do the
planets move?**

the solar system and you have a set of
rigid hoops to represent the orbits of
the planets. If you simply laid the hoops
flat on a table, one inside the other, you
would have a fairly accurate model of
the paths of the planets. To make the
model accurate you would have to tilt
some of the hoops a little bit. But the
remarkable fact is that the planets
move so nearly in the same plane.

The distances between the planets are
greater the farther they are from the
sun. This increase in the distance from
the orbit of each planet to the next one
is regular for the four closest to the sun.
But then between Mars and Jupiter the
gap appears too big.

A German astronomer named Bode
in the eighteenth century worked out a
series of numbers representing the distances of the planets from the sun. He
discovered that Jupiter, the fifth planet
from the sun, was in the orbit where the
sixth planet ought to be. There was no
planet between Mars and Jupiter where
the fifth planet ought to be, according
to his figures.

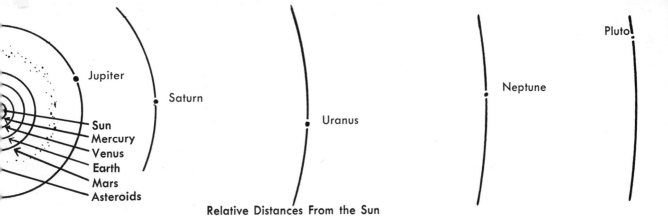

Relative Distances From the Sun

Bode was sure there must be another planet in that area. Finally, in 1801, a tiny body was discovered in orbit between Mars and Jupiter. It was named Ceres. Since then, more than 1,500 other tiny bodies have been discovered in this region. They are called asteroids. Ceres, the largest, is only 480 miles across. Many of them are a mile or less across.

How were the asteroids discovered?

Ever since the motion of the solar system has been understood, men have wondered how it all began. Obviously the sun and its planets must be closely related, since they all move together in such an orderly scheme. By studying the light from the sun and planets, astronomers have been able to tell pretty well what they are made of. They have not been able to detect any material anywhere in the solar system that is not also found on

How did the solar system begin?

earth. In fact, one of the chemical elements, helium, the gas that is used in toy balloons, was discovered in the sun before it was found on earth.

Everything points to the fact that the sun and planets were created from the same stuff. Scientists figure there are two ways the solar system could have begun. The earlier theory holds that it began with a great cloud of whirling gases. The attraction of gravity drew the atoms of the gas closer together. As the gas condensed into a ball, the circular motion increased. Rings of matter were left spinning around the central mass. These condensed to form the planets and the central ball of gas became the sun.

The other main theory, which now seems more likely, is that a star either passed close to the sun or collided with it. This tore a great stream of material from the sun and sent it spinning around. Some of this material was moving too fast to fall back into the sun. It came together to form the planets.

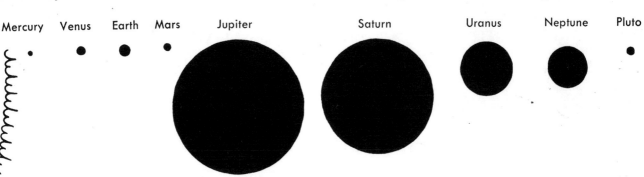

Relative Sizes

EARTH AND MOON

THE PLANET of most interest to us is our own earth. By a small margin, earth is the largest of the terrestrial planets, which makes it fifth in size of all the nine. The first thing an observer on another planet — say, Venus — would notice about the earth is its moon. In fact, from Venus, earth and moon would appear as two planets close together.

During the past few years, everyone has become familiar with the term satellite. The moon was the first satellite that men knew of. A satellite, as we all know since man has put his own satellites in the sky, is a body that orbits around a larger body. The planets are satellites of the sun and the moon is a satellite of the earth. We shall see that other planets also have satellites. But none of the planets has a satellite so large compared with itself as our moon is compared with the earth. The moon is more than one fourth as large as the earth in diameter.

What is a satellite?

The most important thing to remember about the motion of the moon is that it rotates once on its axis as it revolves once about the earth. This is important because it means we have never seen but one side of the moon. It may not be immediately obvious why this is so, but you can demonstrate it to yourself easily enough. Take some object like a jar, with a label on one side, to represent the moon. Move it in a circle around another object — say, a milk bottle — so that the label is always facing the bottle. You will find that to keep the label of the jar facing the milk bottle you will have to rotate the jar slowly. This rotation will amount to one complete turn as your "moon"

Why can we see only one side of the moon?

makes one complete trip around the "earth." It is not just chance that has produced this neat coincidence between the moon's rotation and its revolution. The moon's rotation has been slowed to this speed by the pull of the earth's gravity on it.

The most noticeable thing about the moon as we see it from the earth is its apparently changing shape. From a thin crescent it grows thicker night after night until it becomes a full, round disk. Then it starts shrinking until it finally disappears entirely. The changes in its apparent shape are called phases of the moon. It takes 29½ days for the moon to go through all its phases — for example, from one full moon to the next. From this period come the months of our calendar.

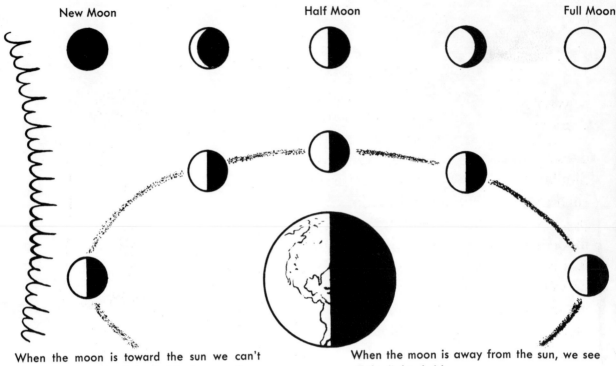

New Moon   Half Moon   Full Moon

When the moon is toward the sun we can't see it, because the lighted side is away from the earth.

When the moon is away from the sun, we see all the lighted side.

Of course, the moon doesn't really change shape during every month. It remains a globe. The light that seems to shine from the moon is the light of the sun shining on the moon's surface and reflected to us on earth. If you take a ball and shine a flashlight on it in a dim room, you will see that half the ball is lighted and half is dark. So it is with the moon — and, for that matter, all the planets as well. Half the moon is always in sunlight and half in the dark. We can see only the part of the moon that is in sunlight. And most of the time we can't see all of that half. The diagram shows hows the different views we get of the moon make it appear to go through its different phases as it orbits around the earth.

Why does the moon "wax" and "wane"?

Notice in the drawing that half the earth is also always lighted by the sun.

Sunlight reflects from the earth to the moon just as it does from the moon to the earth. When the moon is a thin crescent, you can see faintly the dark part of it. It is "earthlight" — sunlight reflected from the earth — that lights the dark part of the moon. In fact, when men reach the moon, they will be able to see the earth go through phases from "new earth" to "full earth."

Looking at the diagram of the moon's phases, you might wonder why, at the time of the new moon, it doesn't come between the earth and sun and cast its shadow on the earth. Similarly, it would seem that at full moon the earth would block the sun's rays from the moon. The reason this doesn't ordinarily happen is that the path of the moon around the earth is not in the same plane as the path of the earth around the sun. The moon is usually "above" or "below" a direct line from sun to earth.

ECLIPSES

This is a solar eclipse, when the moon casts its shadow on earth.

What is an eclipse? But the moon must pass through the plane of the earth's orbit as it circles the earth. Therefore, the moon does occasionally cast its shadow on us. Similarly the earth sometimes casts its shadow on the moon. When this happens, it is called an eclipse. When the moon gets between us and the sun, it is a solar eclipse. When the earth gets between the sun and the moon, it is a lunar eclipse. When the shadow completely cuts off the sun's light, the eclipse is called total; when the shadow only partly hides the face of the sun, it is called a partial eclipse. A total solar eclipse is seen only by people who are in the area of the earth covered by the moon's shadow. This area is rarely more than 150 miles across at any moment and may be a mere point. But the shadow moves across the face of the earth as the moon moves and the earth rotates.

Astronomers sometimes have to travel to strange parts of the earth to

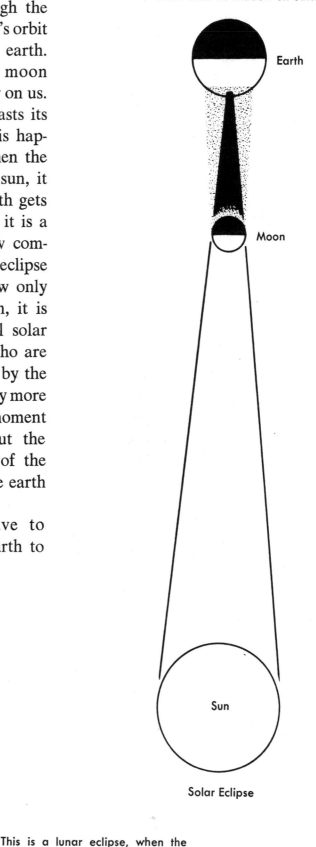

Solar Eclipse

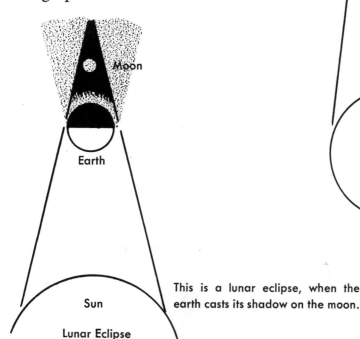

Lunar Eclipse

This is a lunar eclipse, when the earth casts its shadow on the moon.

watch an eclipse of the sun. The last total eclipse visible in the United States was in 1954. The moon's shadow touched the earth in Nebraska and moved through eastern Canada. On July 20, 1963, a total eclipse will be visible in northern Maine. At any one point a total eclipse lasts no more than about eight minutes and may be much shorter. But it is one of the most impressive sights in nature. Imagine the sun blotted out until all that can be seen is a shimmering halo around the black disk of the moon. Some of the brighter stars suddenly appear in the gloomy sky.

Lunar eclipses, when the shadow of the earth darkens the moon, are more frequent than eclipses of the sun. An average of about one total lunar eclipse a year has been visible somewhere in the United States during the past ten years. The moon doesn't quite disappear during such an eclipse because our atmosphere bends a little light around the earth so that the shadow falling on the moon is not quite black.

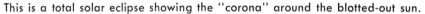

This is a total solar eclipse showing the "corona" around the blotted-out sun.

OUR NEAREST NEIGHBOR

Our nearest neighbor in space, the moon, appears to be made of rock, not much different from the rocky part of the earth. Indeed, it must have come from the same source as the earth. Some scientists think it was actually torn from the earth, leaving the basin of the Pacific Ocean.

What is the moon made of?

Since, on the average, it is less than 235,000 miles from the surface of the earth, we can make out some features of the moon's landscape, even without a telescope. With the largest telescopes, the magnified image of the moon is equivalent to what you could see with the unaided eyes at a distance of less than 200 miles. This is near enough to make out objects only a few hundred feet apart. You can go exploring on the moon with almost any telescope that can be firmly supported. Even field glasses show some of the major features.

Accounts of what the first men to land on the moon will find are so common that the "geography" of the moon is becoming more familiar than some parts of the earth. We all know that the explorers will find no atmosphere, no air or other gases. We know that the sky will be black, with both sun and stars shining at the same time by day. Men will weigh less, because the gravity of the moon is less than that of the earth. And we know that they will find no plants or animals and no soil. The moon is an utter desert.

The moon's physical features have been

**What is the
"Man in the Moon"?**

known for centuries. Galileo was the first to train a telescope on it and see its landscape in detail, but centuries earlier men had named the major features that make up the pattern we see as "the man in the moon." These most noticeable features are broad dark areas, more or less circular. The earliest observers thought they were seas and gave them fanciful Latin names like the Sea of Serenity *(Mare Serenitatis)*, Sea of Storms *(Mare Imbrium)* and Bay of

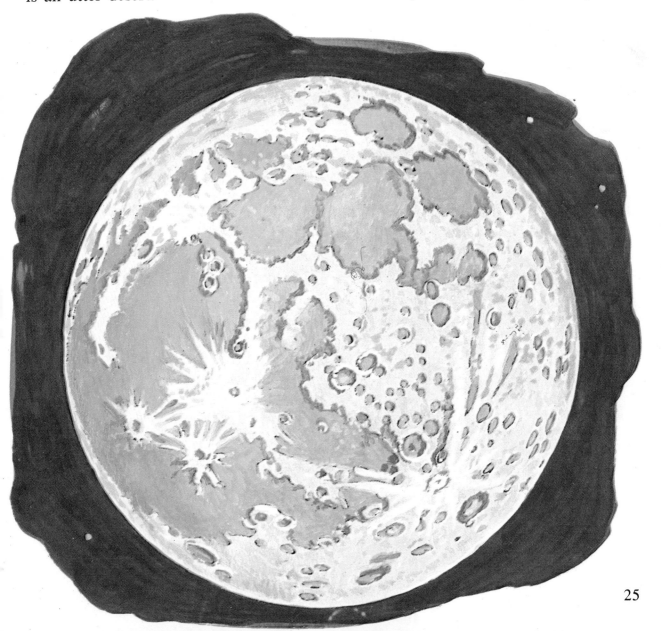

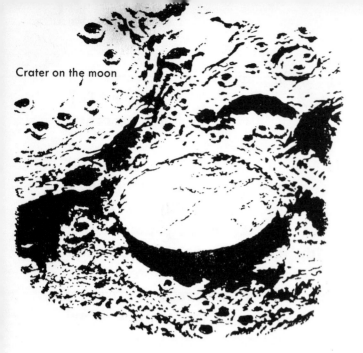
Crater on the moon

Rainbows (*Sinus Iridum*). These dark blotches cover about half of the moon's surface. We now know there is no water on the moon. The areas called seas are broad plains, possibly of hardened volcanic lava and probably covered with dust and gravel. Around these plains the landscape of the moon is extremely rugged, with craggy mountains rising above the plains nearly as high as Mount Everest.

These mountains are made up of craters, which make the moon look like a giant's battlefield. There are two theories about the formation of the craters — one, that they were formed by meteors striking the moon; and, two, that they are extinct volcanoes. It may be that both forces have been at work.

There are also cracks in the surface called rills. These probably opened up as the moon cooled. And there are the mysterious rays. These are white streaks from some of the craters. They run across mountains and plains, in some cases as far as 1,500 miles. They may be dust scattered by whatever explosions produced the craters.

What causes the tides? The moon has important effects on the earth. The chief of these is the tides of the oceans. Tides are caused by the pull of the moon and, to a lesser extent, of the sun. The moon pulls the earth out of shape as shown in the illustration. As the earth rotates, these bulges in the oceans move around the earth causing two high tides and two low tides every day at points on the shore. The pull of the moon, along with that of the sun, makes the earth wobble as it spins, which makes no end of complications in the calculations of astronomers.

Since we live on the earth, the study of the planet itself does not come under the science of astronomy. Because of the wealth of information available, its study is divided among a number of other sciences. However, the astronomer is concerned with the motions of the earth in space. These motions are of the greatest practical importance to us. They produce night and day, the seasons, and our calendar. Knowledge of them is necessary for time-keeping and navigation.

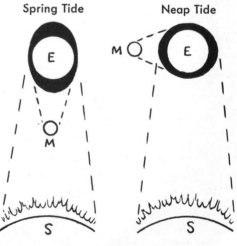

Tides are greater when the sun and moon are in a line, because the gravity of both acts together. These are spring tides. Smaller "neap" tides occur when the moon is at half phase.

DAYS AND SEASONS

"As different as night and day" is an old
saying that illus-

**What causes
night and day?**

trates how basic
this daily change is
to human life. Night and day are produced by the earth's rotation on its axis.
We have said the the sun is always shining on half the earth, while the other
half, away from the sun, is dark. Since
the earth rotates, a point on it moves
through the light and the dark every
day. The rotation is from west to east.
Therefore, New York moves into the
light every day about four hours before

San Francisco reaches the dividing line
between dark and light.

Since the division between daylight
and dark that you see in the drawing is
a sharp line, you might suppose that
dawn and dark would come instantly.
That is exactly what does happen on a
body like the moon which has no air.
On earth the layer of air bends the sun's
light and scatters it so that the sky remains light for a while after the sun
goes down and grows light before the
sun appears.

We tend to think of our twenty-four

The axis of the earth (red arrows) is tilted with reference to the plane of its orbit (yellow band). This causes unequal days and nights over most of the world.

hour day as being divided about equally between darkness and light, but this is true only for people who live on the equator. Elsewhere in the world a day may vary anywhere from six months to a few minutes of actual sunlight. This happens because the earth is tilted. Think of a plane, a flat sheet, running through the center of the earth and the center of the sun. You might suppose that the earth's axis would stick straight up and down through the plane, which would cut the earth in two at the equator. But it doesn't. The equator is tilted at an angle of 23½ degrees to the plane; the earth's axis leans over that much. As the earth revolves around the sun,

sometimes the North Pole is toward the sun, and sometimes the South Pole.

On page 29, you can see that when the North Pole is toward the sun, the circle of sunlight never touches the South Pole, and the other way around. Thus, days and nights in the Arctic and Antarctic are each six months long — half the time it takes the earth to go around the sun. In the Temperate Zone, where we live, we get day and night every twenty-four hours; but the length of time we are in the circle of light is longer or shorter, according to the season. We have long days in summer; short days in winter. At the equator, days and nights are each twelve hours.

The tilt of the earth's axis causes the seasons of the year. You can see below that as the earth moves around the sun, one pole or the other is pointed more toward the sun. When the North Pole is toward the sun, we have summer north of the equator, and people living south of the equator have winter. When the South Pole is pointing toward the sun, it is summer south of the equator, and we have winter. At the beginning of spring and again at the beginning of fall, neither of the two poles is toward the sun.

Why do we have seasons?

The rays of the sun are more concentrated toward the center of the circle of sunlight on the earth. In summer we pass closer to the center of the circle of sunlight. We are also exposed to more sunlight each day in summer. This is because we pass through the circle of sunlight nearer its widest part. This is why summer is warmer than winter. The distance of the earth from the sun has nothing to do with the seasons. In fact, the earth is closer to the sun during our northern winter than in summer.

As the earth moves around the sun, one pole or the other is pointed more toward the sun, because the earth's axis is tilted. The slight change in distance from the earth to the sun during the year is not shown, because it has nothing to do with the seasons.

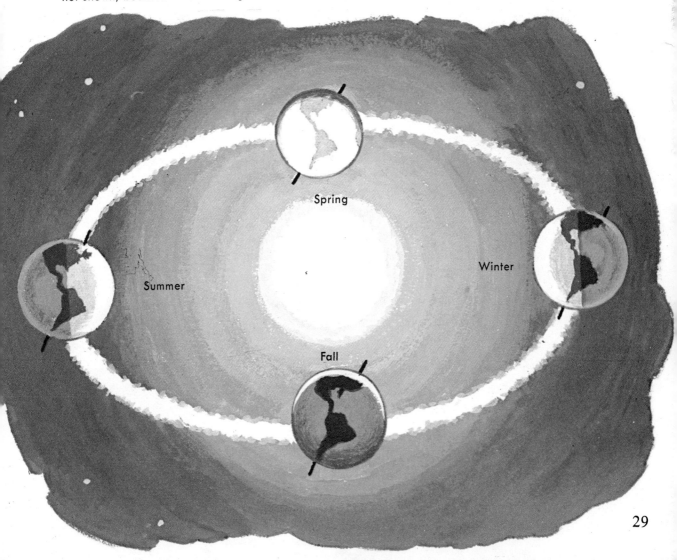

Spring

Summer

Winter

Fall

THE MAN FROM MARS

We know that other planets also have days and nights and seasons. One of the questions

Is there life on other planets?

that has always proved fascinating to almost everybody is whether there are creatures on any of these other worlds to see these changes. The "man from Mars" has become one of the most popular subjects for jokes. Why Mars? We naturally expect that if life exists on other planets it would be on those most like the earth. These are Mars and Venus, the two planets nearest to us. Venus is toward the sun and Mars is in the other direction.

Of the two, the nearest planet Venus is more like the earth in size and distance from the sun, but Mars has excited more interest because we can see its surface. Venus is covered with clouds that we can't penetrate, even with rays that enable us to take pictures through earth clouds.

Mars was named for the god of war because of its red color, which is plain even to our unaided eyes. When Mars is closest to the earth and sunlight is reflected directly from it, a very modest telescope will enlarge it to the apparent size of the moon. Although we can't see its features as clearly as the moon's, we have been able to learn more about its surface than about any other object in the sky except the moon.

Mars through a telescope

The most noticeable features of Mars

What are the effects of seasons on Mars?

as seen through a telescope are the ice caps at its north and south poles. These appear just as those on earth would to a man on Mars. Since Mars is tilted at about the same angle that earth is, it has seasons as we do. The effect of the seasons can be clearly seen in the growing and shrinking of the polar ice caps. Another seasonal change has convinced most astronomers that there is some form of plant life in low-lying areas. These areas change from blue-green in summer to brown in winter. Seasonal changes also are accompanied by an effect that looks much as if water flowed into these areas of vegetation from the polar caps as they melt.

A great argument raged among scientists for many years about these markings. Some saw straight canals connecting "oases," from which they concluded that there must be intelligent creatures on Mars who had dug the canals to irrigate their lands. Astronomers at present are very doubtful about these canals, but they do agree that it appears as if moisture — perhaps in the form of vapor — comes down from the polar caps and seems to nourish plant life. They also agree that the lighter areas, which give Mars its red color, are deserts of rusty rocks. They have not been able to detect enough oxygen in the atmosphere to support animal life as we know it, but they do find evidence that both water and oxygen were once plentiful. It is quite possible that there once were creatures on Mars, and it is conceivable that they are still there. But they would have had to find a way to produce life-giving oxygen and water from the rocks by chemical means and also a way to keep warm during the planet's sub-zero nights.

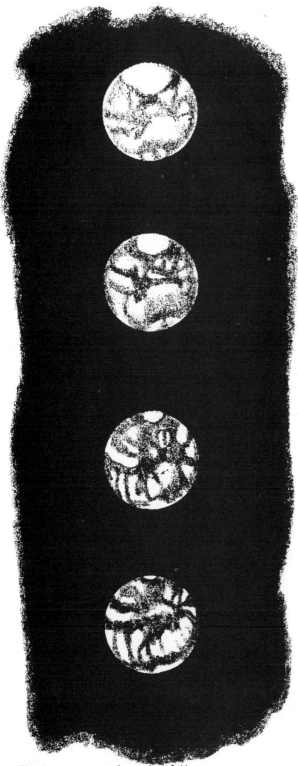

The ice cap over the pole of Mars shrinks and grows with the seasons.

31

THE MYSTERY OF VENUS

THE OTHER most earthlike planet, Venus, is wrapped in the mystery of its clouds. Because we can't see its surface, we can't even observe whether Venus rotates. Scientists, however, have figured out by other means that it almost certainly does rotate, though very slowly. A Venusian day is probably about as long as our month.

Because clouds reflect light better than rocks, Venus is the

Why is Venus so bright?

brightest object in the sky aside from the sun and the moon. It can often be seen even in daylight; and at night it is sometimes bright enough to cast faint shadows on earth.

In some ways, such as the range of temperature, Venus seems a more likely home than Mars for creatures like us. The big question has been the nature of Venus's clouds, which were long thought to be made of material that would make life on the surface impossible. However, in 1959, observations from a balloon 15 miles above the earth showed evidence of water vapor in the planet's clouds. Since earth clouds are made of water vapor, the discovery opened new possibilities of life on Venus.

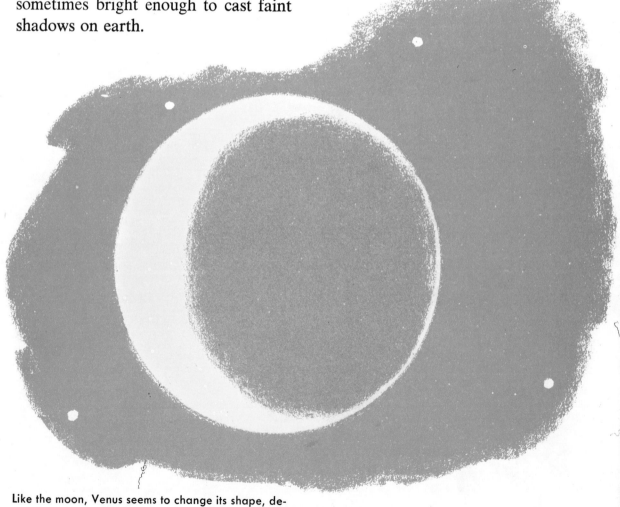

Like the moon, Venus seems to change its shape, depending on its position relative to the sun and earth.

MERCURY AND PLUTO

BEYOND VENUS, toward the sun, Mercury orbits about 36,000,000 miles from the sun. No question has ever been raised about the possibility of life on Mercury. It has the most extreme conditions of any of the planets. Like the moon, Mercury's period of rotation and revolution are equal so that it presents the same side to the sun at all times, just as the moon presents the same side to the earth.

Since it is so close to the sun and has

What are conditions on Mercury?

no atmosphere, the side toward the sun is always hot enough to melt lead, while the dark side is about as cold as cold can be — that is, close to absolute zero. The surface of Mercury is probably much like the surface of the moon. Indeed, as the smallest planet, it is only about one third bigger in diameter than our moon.

Mercury is difficult to observe, because it is never very far above the horizon at night. Astronomers observe it in the daytime, using special screens.

The other planet that is classified as a "terrestrial" planet is Pluto, farthest from the sun. We know little about this planet, which was only discovered in 1930. Astronomers have figured out that it evidently has no atmosphere, and it may be made of black rock. It is bound to be extremely cold so far from the sun. Air would turn liquid.

THE GIANT PLANETS

To an astronomer just outside the solar system, all the planets we have described — Mercury, Venus, Earth, Mars and Pluto — would be insignificant. He would regard the system of planets as composed of mainly the four giants: Jupiter, Saturn, Uranus and Neptune. If he knew of the earthlike planets, he would probably think of them as minor fragments, much as we regard the asteroids.

With the curious exception of Pluto, the earthlike planets and the giants are neatly divided by the asteroid belt, three small planets huddled inside this band and the giants spread out beyond.

How big is the planet Jupiter? Jupiter, the first planet beyond the asteroids, is the dominant planet of the whole system. Jupiter would hold more than a thousand earths. The earth is not as big compared to Jupiter as Jupiter is compared to the sun itself. Its diameter is more than one-tenth the sun's. But like the sun, Jupiter is not nearly so dense as the earth. Astronomers are fairly certain that Jupiter consists of a rocky core surrounded by deep layers of gases.

As befits the largest planet, Jupiter has the largest family of satellites. Twelve moons have been discovered.

The clouds of Jupiter show changing patterns.

Saturn

These range in size from one as small as ten miles in diameter to one larger than the planet Mercury! Jupiter and its satellites form a system comparable to the sun and its planets, except that Jupiter does not provide its own light. Far from it — Jupiter is bitter cold. Its surface temperature has been measured at 216 degrees below zero.

The other giant planets — Saturn, Uranus, and Neptune — are similar to Jupiter in make-up. Uranus and Neptune are less than half as big in diameter, but Saturn's diameter is more than three-quarters the size of Jupiter's. Saturn is the least dense of any of the planets. It is lighter than water.

What are the rings of Saturn?

Saturn is the most spectacular planet of all to see through a telescope. This is because of its remarkable rings. These are bright, thin bands around the equator of the planet. The entire ring system is 171,000 miles across from the outer to the inner edge, but probably no more than ten miles thick. It has been determined that the rings are made up of separate tiny particles, each moving in its own orbit. They are probably particles of ice of different sizes, many smaller than an ice cube. Saturn boasts nine satellites in addition to its rings.

Uranus and Neptune are very similar to Jupiter, though much smaller. They also have satellites — Uranus five and Neptune two.

METEORS AND COMETS

THE PLANETS and their satellites do not complete the sun's family. There is an unknown number of smaller particles, possibly fragments left over from the formation of the solar system. These particles seem to move mostly in swarms with a few strays scattered about.

Meteors

The most frequent evidence we see of them is "shooting stars." These are fragments called

What are "shooting stars"?

meteors that are swept into the earth's atmosphere as we travel through space. They are moving so fast that friction with the air causes them to glow white hot, and they burn up, usually long before they near the earth, When a fragment does reach the earth, it is called a meteorite. A number of large meteorites have been known to strike the earth; one in Arizona produced a crater 4,000 feet across.

Some of these swarms of fragments have orbits that take them so close to the sun at one point that the sun's energy

What are comets?

breaks down the particles and drives gases and dust out behind them in a long glowing tail. These are called comets. Although they have in the past caused widespread panic on the rare occasions when big ones appeared, there is nothing to fear from them. The particles are so tiny and spread out that

Meteorite crater in Arizona. The meteorite apparently exploded when it landed.

the earth could go right through a comet without our knowing it. The paths of most comets are extremely long, flat ellipses, shaped something like a cigar. This means that it takes them a long time to revolve around the sun. The most famous comet, Halley's, shows up about every 76 years. It will be seen again in the year 1987.

All the bodies we have described — planets, asteroids, satellites of planets, meteors, and comets — make up the family of the sun. To us on earth this family is vast and impressive, but from the nearest star, the entire system is just a tiny speck among the countless specks of light in space.

Halley's comet

THE STARS

Our own sun is a star. Every one of the vast number of twinkling points of light in the sky is a gigantic atomic furnace, just as our sun is. And among the stars, our sun is not a particularly impressive example. It is about an average-size star, in between the giants and the dwarfs. (Giant and dwarf are not mere

What are the stars?

figures of speech; they are two classes of stars.) Of course, the sun's system of planets could not even be guessed at from the distance of the nearest stars. At least one of the stars we see as a point of light is itself big enough to contain our entire solar system!

How far away are the stars? The distances are hard to imagine.

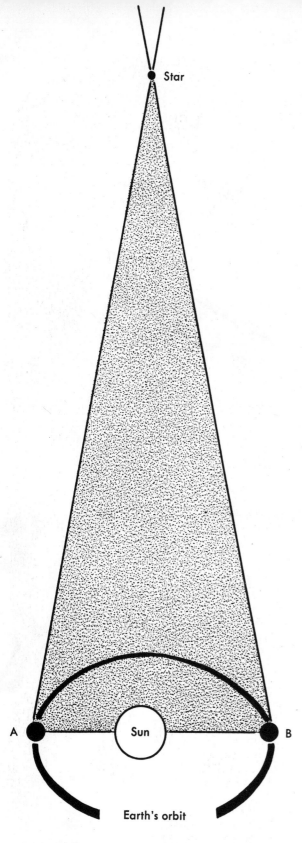

Astronomers measure the distance to a nearer star by observing it from opposite points in the earth's orbit around the sun. By noting the change in the star's apparent position from the two points, they can measure the angles of the triangle shown. Since they know the distance AB, they can calculate the distance to the star by geometry, a branch of mathematics.

The best way to deal with such distances is in terms of time, and that is what astronomers have done. You might say when asked how far you live from school: "About a fifteen-minute walk." Since the only way astronomers know the stars is from their light, they naturally use the speed of light to describe their distances. They say of a star that it is fifteen light-years away. Light moves at just over 186,000 miles per second. In one year it moves just under six trillion miles. Nobody can imagine six trillion miles, but everyone can think of the length of a year. When we look at the nearest star, the brightest star in the constellation Centaurus, we are looking back into time four years. If we should see it explode, we would be watching something that happened four years ago, the time it takes light to reach us from that star. Without using a telescope you can actually see back into time a million and a half years. The farthest light in the sky visible to the unaided eye is the Great Spiral in Andromeda, 1,500,000 light-years away.

At the beginning of the book, when we looked at the sky through the eyes of ancient men, we saw the stars as fixed to a sphere surrounding us. We noted that the brightest of them formed recognizable patterns. By now we know that both the celestial sphere and the constellations are only illusions.

We have seen that the lights of the sky actually come from bodies that vary in distance from a quarter of a million *miles* (the moon) to a million and a

How far away are the stars?

half *light-years* (the Andromeda Spiral). The second thing to note is that the stars that appear to form patterns usually are not close together at all; one may be ten times as far away as another in the same constellation.

Those stars that are brighter are not necessarily any bigger than the others.

Why are some stars brighter than others? A star's brightness depends on three things: its size, its distance, and the kind of star it is. Some stars give off more light than others the same size. The brightest star in our sky, Sirius, is a small star that happens to be relatively close. The closest star is rather bright, but the next closest is invisible without a telescope. The stars were classified in ancient times by how bright they appeared. Ptolemy called this their magnitude. He broke the stars down into six groups, from the brightest (first magnitude) to the faintest (sixth magnitude). There are about 4,000 stars of the first six magnitudes. The term is still in use, but the measurement has been refined and extended until astronomers can speak of a magnitude of 21.3, for example.

One of the things that determines the apparent brightness of a star is the actual intensity of its light. If you watch a piece of iron being melted, you will notice that it first begins to glow a dull red, gradually grows more orange and then yellow and finally white. The colors of the stars indicate in much the same way how hot and, therefore, how bright they are. The red stars are the

39

coolest. The yellow stars, like our sun, are moderately hot in the scale, and the white and blue-white stars are the hottest.

These colors seem to be related also to the size of stars. The biggest stars are red, the stars in the middle range of size are yellow, and the smallest stars are white and blue-white. One of the most interesting things about this range in size is that there is not a tremendous difference in the actual amount of material in the different sizes of stars. The material is more spread out in the large stars and more condensed in the small ones. Ninety per cent of the stars we know about have a mass of not less than one tenth nor more than ten times that of our sun. The range of sizes, however, extends from dwarfs hardly larger than the earth to giants that would hold the entire solar system.

It seems as if the different sizes and colors of stars might represent different stages of development, and that is just what astronomers believe. However, they have not determined what the process is, since stars appear to fall into different groups when they are classified according to their various properties.

One theory is that stars are formed out

How are stars formed? of the clouds of atoms, mostly hydrogen, that are scattered through space. When enough atoms collect, the gravity between them pulls them closer and closer together until they begin to form a ball. As they continue to be squeezed together, they bump against each other so hard that they produce more and more heat, until finally they start the atomic chain reaction that leads them to blaze like the sun. Finally, as it condenses more and more, the star becomes as compact and hot as the white dwarfs.

There is probably a limit to how far this process can go, since the more compressed the atoms are the more active they become from the heat that their collisions generate. Finally there is an explosion and the atoms are again scattered into clouds, from which the process can start all over again. Explosions have been seen that would appear to be just such an end to a star.

A nova, an exploding star.

40

THE MILKY WAY

IN DESCRIBING the solar system, we noted that everything in it was in motion. With the improvement of measuring methods, men have discovered that the stars, which were always thought of as fixed, are also in motion. This real motion of the stars relative to each other should not be confused with the apparent motion due to the earth's rotation. The stars' real motion seems extremely slow to us because they are so far away. Actually, they are moving at tremendous speeds. And our sun is no exception. It appears to be heading at a terrific speed toward a point in the constellation Hercules, carrying all its planets along with it.

Where are the stars going? All those we can see as individual stars are moving round and round in one giant system called a galaxy.

What is the Milky Way? From our position within this system we see the heart of it as a pale white band across our sky

— it is the familiar Milky Way. The Milky Way, as a telescope shows, is composed of stars so close together that they give the appearance of a shining cloud. This is an inside view of our galaxy. From far enough outside, it would look like a fiery pinwheel from one view and like a disk, swollen at the center, from an edgewise view. Our solar system is located well out near the edge of the disk. When we look at the Milky Way in the sky, we are looking toward the center of the disk; consequently, we see stars one behind the other, until they merge together. In a direction away from the Milky Way in the sky, we see only the stars in our own part of the disk, so they appear more widely scattered.

The number of stars in our galaxy has been estimated as high as 200,000,-000,000. It has been shown that the number would have to be more than 30,-000,000,000. The dimensions of the galaxy are somewhere between 100,-000 and 200,000 light-years across, and 10,000 to 20,000 light-years thick at the middle. Our sun is located 35,000 to 50,000 light-years from the center.

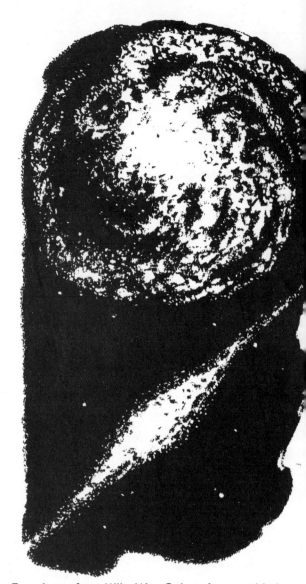

Two views of our Milky Way Galaxy from outside it.

As we said, the whole system is in motion, with all the stars whirling around the center. Our sun would make one revolution around the center in about 250,000,000 years, and this is whirling, considering the distance!

When we look at the Milky Way on a clear, dark night, we notice that there seem to be breaks and holes in the light band. These are not holes, but black clouds of cold star material that black out the stars beyond. It is from this material that we believe new stars are eventually formed.

+ is the position of our solar system in the Milky Way.

THE GALAXIES

What else is in the universe?

Is this galaxy of stars all there is in the universe? Far from it! We have learned that the Milky Way island is but one of countless galaxies like it. The nearest of these, the Great Spiral in Andromeda, can occasionally be seen by the unaided eye. It appears to be almost a twin of our own. In fact, much that we have learned of our own galaxy has been from observing it.

Not all galaxies have a spiral structure, however. Some seem to be formless. These are assumed to be galaxies in the making. Two of these smaller star clouds are very bright in the sky of the far Southern Hemisphere. They were first reported by the explorer Magellan as he rounded South America on man's first trip around the world. Consequently, they are called Magellanic clouds. Other galaxies have a simpler elliptical shape than the spirals. They are assumed to be older and more stable systems. There are also some small "globular clusters" of stars just outside our galaxy.

Even the galaxies themselves seem to be grouped into systems. Beyond our group of about fifteen galaxies there appear to be other groups. One of these groups seems to contain over 1,000 galaxies. On a single photograph made with the 200-inch reflecting telescope at Mount Palomar, more than 10,000 galaxies were detected!

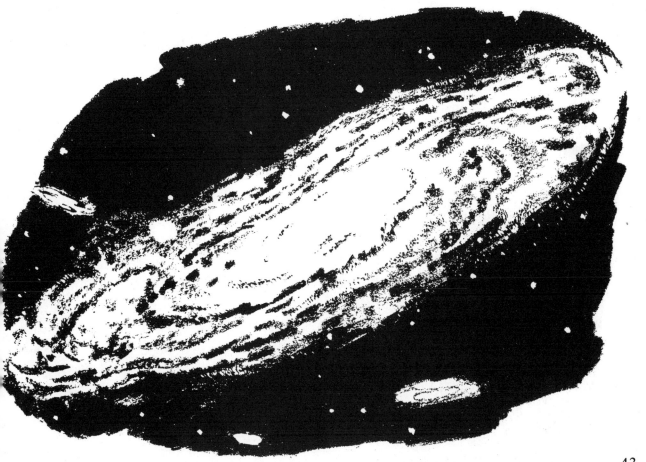

Having found that the planets move in a definite pattern and that the stars move in turn in a pattern in their galaxies, the question naturally arises: do the galaxies themselves move together in some stable pattern of their own? The answer is one of the most astonishing things that science has ever been faced with: the galaxies are apparently all flying away from each other at tremendous speeds and their speeds get greater the farther apart they are!

THE UNIVERSE

What does this mean? Nobody knows,

What is happening to the universe?

but it has produced some of the most fantastic-sounding and yet carefully thought-out pictures of the universe that man has ever conceived.

Most of the theories involve higher mathematics and Einstein's Theory of Relativity. Consequently, it is not possible to explain here how they were arrived at, but in general they take one of two views.

The first is called *evolutionary*. Scientist-philosophers who take this view believe that the universe was created in one giant explosion of one ball of energy; the galaxies created by the explosion are still hurtling outward. Mathematicians are even able to calculate that the explosion took place somewhere between five and eight billion years ago. Some thinkers who agree with this view say that the present is just one stage of a repeating process. At a certain point the process will be reversed and the universe will contract again to one ball, only to explode again. This sounds familiar from the theory we discussed of how stars are made.

The other main view of the universe is called the *steady-state* or *balanced* universe. This view holds that the universe has no beginning and no end, that it always has had and always will have about the same distribution of material. As the galaxies spread out, the material to make new ones is being created at a rate that will balance the loss of the present galaxies. Where will the present ones go? Since they are moving apart faster and faster, they will eventually reach the speed of light. But matter can't go that fast, according to our present theories. Will they just disappear?

When we look up at the stars today, we still feel the wonder that the first man felt.

LET'S GO STAR HUNTING

NOW THAT YOU know the "how" and "why" of the stars, you will want to know them by name. The obvious way to learn the constellations is by consulting a map of them. Charts of the major constellations are printed on the last page of the book. The simple instructions on the page facing this one show you how to mount the charts so that they will be most useful at any place and time.

When mounted, one side of the chart shows the sky as it appears looking north and the other side shows the stars to the south. The straight border of each cardboard mask represents the horizon.

The first thing necessary in learning to use the chart is, curiously enough, to put yourself back in history many centuries and imagine the universe as the ancients conceived it. Think of the sky as a hollow globe with the stars fixed to it and imagine that the globe revolves around the earth at its center.

Once we can picture the sky as a globe, we can fix positions on it by the same means that we describe positions on earth. Everyone has seen a globe map of the earth. If you look at one carefully, you will notice that there are circles drawn on its surface. Some of these circles pass through both the North and South Poles. These are called meridians. The other circles cut the meridians at right angles and go around the earth parallel to each other. These are called parallels of latitude and the

one halfway between the poles is the equator. Both meridians and parallels are numbered so we can describe the location of any spot on earth by naming the meridian and the parallel that pass through it.

We can do the same thing in the sky. We can imagine circles on the celestial sphere that correspond exactly to the same circles on earth. On your chart the circles are parallels of latitude and the straight lines are meridians. The meridians appear as straight lines because the chart is drawn as if we were looking directly at the north and south poles of the sky. If you look straight down at the North Pole of a globe map of the earth, the meridians will look like straight lines running from the pole to the equator. The outer circle of your chart, then, represents the celestial equator.

Now that you have an idea of the "geography" of the sky, you are ready to put your chart to use.

When you set your chart for the date, it will show the sky as it appears about 9 P.M. (10 P.M. Daylight Time). If the hour is later, move it counterclockwise the distance of one meridian for each hour. If the time is earlier than 9 P.M., move it clockwise. This is necessary because the celestial sphere rotates. It turns completely around once every 24 hours. Therefore, in one hour it will have moved the distance between two adjoining meridians on the chart. This rotation is counterclockwise.

45

HOW TO MOUNT THE STAR CHARTS

1. You will need three pieces of heavy cardboard 7½ inches square. On one (cardboard A in the picture), draw a circle in the exact center, setting the compasses at 2¾ inches. Cut out this circle with a sharp blade, taking care not to damage the edge of either the circle or the remaining piece. Smooth the edges with light sandpaper, if necessary, to permit the circle to turn easily when replaced in its hole.

2. Label one of the other pieces of cardboard "North" (this is cardboard B in the picture), and the other "South" (cardboard C). In the center of each draw a circle 2½ inches in radius. Draw a line through the center and parallel to the sides of the cardboard. Now you must find the *latitude* of your home. It will determine the size of the cutouts in cardboards B and C. If you can't find it from a map, your local weather bureau can tell you the latitude of the town. Your latitude in the United States will lie somewhere between about 26 degrees and about 45 degrees. Now convert your latitude into inches for your chart by letting 10 degrees of latitude equal ¼ inch. Thus, if you live in New York City, which is about 41 degrees, your measurement will be just about 1 inch.

3. On cardboard B, labeled "North," measure off your latitude distance along the center line *down* from the center of the circle. At this point draw a line across the circle at right angles to the center line. Everything above this line within the circle is to be cut out, including the notch at the top, shown in the illustration.

4. On cardboard C, labeled "South," measure the same latitude distance *up* from the center of the circle, draw a line at right angles, and cut out the small portion shown above the line, as in the illustration.

5. *After you have read all the instructions* and know clearly how to put the chart together, cut out the star charts from the last page of the book. Paste one chart on each side of the disk cut from cardboard A, matching up the months exactly. With the disk in place in its hole, put the three pieces of cardboard together as shown, with the cutouts of B and C both at the top. Tape the edges together or glue the three pieces together at the edges. Make sure the circle turns easily. Label the horizon and celestial equator as shown. Instructions for using the chart are on page 45.

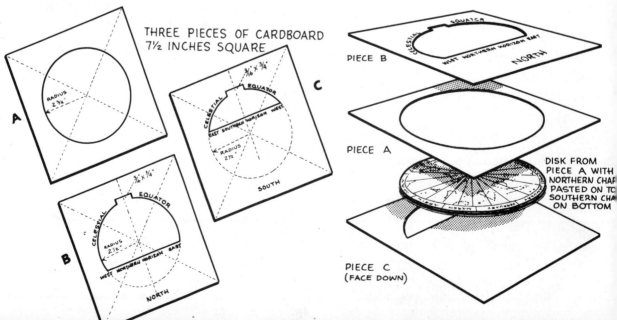

THREE PIECES OF CARDBOARD 7½ INCHES SQUARE

PIECE B

PIECE A

PIECE C (FACE DOWN)

DISK FROM PIECE A WITH NORTHERN CHART PASTED ON TO SOUTHERN CHART ON BOTTOM

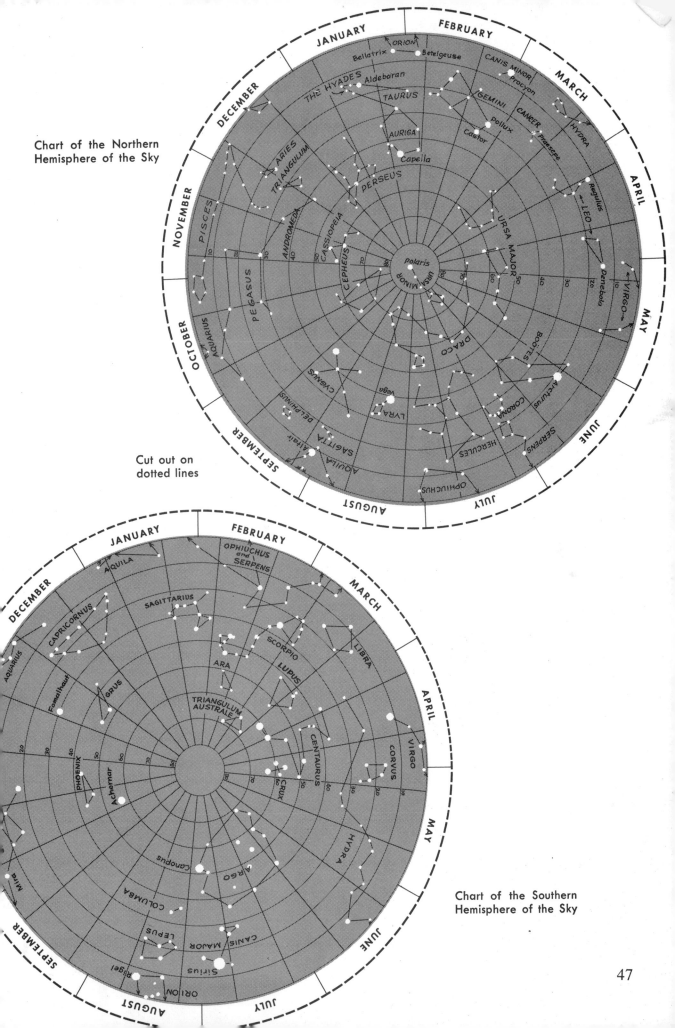

Chart of the Northern Hemisphere of the Sky

Cut out on dotted lines

Chart of the Southern Hemisphere of the Sky

47

910 F.W.